THE SECRET LIFE OF A CEO

By Harry Holland

TABLE OF CONTENTS

CHAPTER 1: INTRODUCTION

"The function of leadership is to produce more leaders, not more followers." - Ralph Nader

The role of a CEO is one of the most critical and challenging positions in any organization. A CEO is responsible for setting the strategic direction of the company, making major decisions, managing resources, and leading the company's employees towards success. However, the secret life of a CEO is not always fully understood by those outside of the executive suite. In this chapter, we will explore what it means to be a CEO, the challenges they face, and the importance of understanding the secret life of a CEO.

A CEO, or Chief Executive Officer, is the highest-ranking executive in an organization. They are responsible for the overall performance and success of the company. This includes setting the strategic direction of the company, making major decisions, managing resources, and overseeing the work of other executives and employees.

The CEO is also responsible for representing the company to external stakeholders, including investors, customers, and the public. They are the face of the company and must be able to effectively communicate the company's values and mission.

The Secret Life of a CEO is a book that provides a comprehensive look at what it means to be a CEO. It covers everything from the early life of a CEO to their leadership style, work-life balance, decision-making, managing a team, crisis management, corporate social responsibility, communication skills, innovation, managing finances, networking, maintaining a positive reputation, and personal growth and development.

The book aims to give readers a better understanding of the secret life of a CEO, including the challenges they face, the strategies they use to overcome these challenges, and the personal and professional growth they experience along the way.

Understanding the secret life of a CEO is essential for several reasons. Firstly, CEOs play a critical role in shaping the direction of their companies and making decisions that impact the lives of their employees, customers, and shareholders. Therefore, understanding their thought processes, leadership styles, and decision-making criteria can provide valuable insights into how successful companies operate.

Secondly, understanding the secret life of a CEO can also provide aspiring leaders with insights into the skills, experiences, and attributes required to become a successful CEO. By learning about the challenges CEOs face and how they overcome them, aspiring leaders can better prepare themselves for a future in executive leadership.

Lastly, understanding the secret life of a CEO can help employees at all levels of the organization better understand the motivations and decision-making criteria of their leaders. This can lead to more effective communication, increased trust, and a more positive and productive work environment.

The secret life of a CEO is essential for anyone interested in leadership, business, or organizational behavior. By exploring the topics covered in this book, readers can gain valuable insights into the challenges and strategies used by successful CEOs, and use this knowledge to enhance their own leadership skills and career prospects.

CHAPTER 2: EARLY LIFE OF A CEO

"The only way to do great work is to love what you do." - Steve Jobs

The journey to becoming a CEO is often a long and winding road. Many successful CEOs did not start out with the intention of becoming the leader of a company. Instead, their early life experiences, education, and career choices led them down a path that ultimately prepared them for the role of CEO. In this chapter, we will explore the early life experiences of successful CEOs and how these experiences prepared them for executive leadership.

Childhood experiences can play a significant role in shaping the values, beliefs, and motivations of an individual. Many successful CEOs credit their childhood experiences as a critical factor in their development as leaders.

For example, Jeff Bezos, the founder, and CEO of Amazon, grew up on a ranch in Texas, where he learned the value of hard work and resourcefulness. As a child, Bezos would often help his grandfather on the farm, where he learned the importance of problem-solving and perseverance.

Similarly, Mary Barra, the CEO of General Motors, grew up in a working-class family and learned the importance of teamwork and collaboration from her father, who was a die maker at a General Motors plant.

Education and early career experiences can also play a critical role in preparing individuals for executive leadership. Many successful CEOs hold advanced degrees, such as an MBA, and have experience working in a variety of roles and industries.

For example, Satya Nadella, the CEO of Microsoft, holds an MBA from the University of Chicago Booth School of Business and has worked in a variety of roles at Microsoft, including leading the company's cloud computing division.

Similarly, Indra Nooyi, the former CEO of PepsiCo, holds an MBA from the Yale School of Management and has worked in a variety of roles at PepsiCo, including leading the company's international business and overseeing the acquisition of Tropicana.

The first steps towards becoming a CEO are often taken early in one's career. Many successful CEOs started out in entry-level positions and worked their way up through the ranks, gaining valuable experience and skills along the way.

Doug McMillon, the CEO of Walmart, started out as a summer associate at the company while he was still in college. He worked his way up through the company, holding a variety of positions, including store manager and buyer, before ultimately being named CEO.

Sheryl Sandberg, the COO of Facebook, started out as an entry-level employee at the World Bank and worked her way up through the ranks, eventually becoming the Chief of Staff to the U.S. Treasury Secretary and the Vice President of Global Online Sales and Operations at Google before joining Facebook.

The early life experiences of successful CEOs are often critical in preparing them for the challenges of executive leadership. Childhood experiences can instill important values such as hard work, perseverance, and teamwork, while education and early career experiences can provide valuable knowledge and skills.

The experiences gained through entry-level positions can be critical in providing individuals with a comprehensive understanding of the inner workings of an organization. This can include knowledge of key business processes, industry trends, and customer needs, all of which are critical in developing effective business strategies and making key decisions.

The early life experiences of successful CEOs are often critical in preparing them for executive leadership. Childhood experiences, education, and early career experiences can instill important values, provide valuable knowledge and skills, and develop a comprehensive understanding of the inner workings of an organization. By understanding the early life experiences of successful CEOs, aspiring leaders can gain valuable insights into the skills and attributes required to become a successful CEO.

CHAPTER 3: DEVELOPING LEADERSHIP SKILLS

"Leadership is not about being in charge. It's about taking care of those in your charge." - Simon Sinek

Leadership skills are critical for anyone who aspires to be a CEO. Effective leadership is not a static trait; it is something that can be developed and honed over time. In this chapter, we will explore the key skills required for effective leadership and how aspiring CEOs can develop these skills.

Visionary thinking is a critical skill for effective leadership. A CEO must be able to see beyond the current state of the organization and develop a long-term vision for the future. This requires a deep understanding of the industry, the competitive landscape, and emerging trends.

One way to develop visionary thinking is to regularly read industry publications and attend conferences and networking events. By staying up-to-date on the latest trends and developments, aspiring CEOs can develop a more comprehensive understanding of the industry and the challenges and opportunities it presents.

Strategic planning is another critical skill for effective leadership. A CEO must be able to develop and execute a comprehensive strategy that aligns with the organization's long-term vision. This requires a deep understanding of the organization's strengths and weaknesses, as well as the competitive landscape and emerging trends.

Another way to develop strategic planning skills is to participate in business case competitions or simulations. These activities provide an opportunity to develop and execute a comprehensive strategy, as well as receive feedback from industry experts and peers.

An action to develop effective communication skills is to participate in public speaking or debate competitions. These activities provide an opportunity to practice articulating ideas and concepts in a clear and concise manner, as well as develop the ability to think on one's feet and respond to unexpected questions or challenges.

Effective communication is a fundamental skill for effective leadership. A CEO must be able to communicate effectively with employees, customers, investors, and other stakeholders. This requires the ability to clearly articulate ideas and concepts, listen actively, and provide feedback in a constructive manner.

Team building is another critical skill for effective leadership. A CEO must be able to build and lead a high-performing team that can execute the organization's strategy effectively. This requires the ability to identify and recruit top talent, foster a culture of collaboration and innovation, and provide opportunities for professional development and growth.

Team building skills can be developed by participating in team sports or group projects. These activities provide an opportunity to practice working collaboratively with others towards a common goal, as well as develop the ability to identify and leverage individual strengths and weaknesses to achieve optimal performance.

Conflict resolution is also critical skill for effective leadership. A CEO must be able to manage conflicts and disputes effectively, whether they arise between employees, customers, or other stakeholders. This requires the ability to identify the root cause of conflicts, listen actively, and provide constructive feedback and solutions.

Of course, one way to develop conflict resolution skills is to participate in negotiation or mediation training. These activities provide an opportunity to practice managing conflicts and disputes in a controlled environment, as well as develop the ability to identify and leverage common interests and goals to reach mutually beneficial solutions.

Emotional intelligence is a critical skill for effective leadership. A CEO must be able to understand and manage their own emotions, as well as the emotions of others. This requires the ability to empathize with others, build strong relationships, and provide support and guidance when needed.

Developing emotional intelligence can be through participating in leadership development programs or workshops. These activities provide an opportunity to learn about the principles and practices of emotional intelligence, as well as develop the ability to apply them in a real-world context.

Developing effective leadership skills is critical for anyone who aspires to be a CEO. Visionary thinking, strategic planning, effective communication, team building, conflict resolution, and emotional intelligence are all key skills that can be developed and honed.

CHAPTER 4: BUILDING AND MAINTAINING A STRONG COMPANY CULTURE

: "Culture is the widening of the mind and of the spirit." - Jawaharlal Nehru

Company culture is a critical factor in the success of any organization. A strong and positive culture can attract and retain top talent, foster innovation and creativity, and drive business growth. In this chapter, we will explore the key elements of a strong company culture and how CEOs can build and maintain a culture that supports their vision and mission.

The first step in building a strong company culture is to define what it means for the organization. This involves articulating the organization's core values, beliefs, and behaviors that reflect its unique identity and purpose. The CEO should work with their leadership team to develop a clear and concise statement that defines the company culture and communicates it to all employees.

Once the company culture has been defined, it is important to communicate it effectively to all employees. This includes not only the values and behaviors that are expected, but also the purpose and vision that the culture supports. The CEO should ensure that the company culture is embedded in all aspects of the organization, from recruitment and onboarding to performance management and rewards.

Building and maintaining a strong company culture requires commitment and leadership from the CEO and senior leadership team. The CEO should lead by example, modeling the behaviors and values that are expected of all employees. This includes being transparent, honest, and ethical in all business dealings, as well as demonstrating a commitment to employee development and engagement.

Employee engagement is a critical factor in building and maintaining a strong company culture. Engaged employees are more productive, more committed to the organization, and more likely to stay with the organization over the long term. The CEO should develop strategies to foster employee engagement, such as providing opportunities for career development, offering flexible work arrangements, and recognizing and rewarding employee contributions.

Innovation and creativity are essential for organizational growth and success. A strong company culture should encourage and support innovation and creativity, and provide employees with the resources and support they need to develop new ideas and solutions. The CEO should create an environment that rewards risk-taking and experimentation, and provides employees with the freedom and autonomy to explore new ideas and approaches.

Celebrating successes and learning from failures is an important part of building and maintaining a strong company culture. The CEO should recognize and celebrate employee achievements and successes, and use them as examples of the behaviors and values that are expected of all employees. At the same time, the CEO should acknowledge and learn from failures and setbacks, using them as opportunities to identify areas for improvement and to reinforce the importance of continuous learning and growth.

A diverse and inclusive culture is critical for organizational success. A diverse workforce brings a variety of perspectives and experiences that can lead to more innovative and effective solutions. The CEO should develop strategies to build a diverse and inclusive culture, such as recruiting from a wide range of talent pools, providing training and development programs that address unconscious bias, and creating an environment where everyone feels valued and respected.

Maintaining a strong company culture requires ongoing effort and attention. The CEO should regularly review and assess the culture, and make adjustments as needed to ensure that it continues to support the organization's vision and mission. This may involve revisiting the company's core values and behaviors, providing additional resources and support for employee development and engagement, or introducing new initiatives to support innovation and creativity.

Building and maintaining a strong company culture is critical for organizational success. Defining the company culture, communicating it effectively, leading by example, fostering employee engagement, encouraging innovation and creativity, celebrating successes and learning from failures, building a diverse and inclusive culture, and maintaining the culture over time are all key elements that CEOs should focus on. By doing so, they can attract and retain top talent, drive business growth, and create a workplace culture that employees are proud to be a part of.

CHAPTER 5: EFFECTIVE
COMMUNICATION FOR CEOS

: "The art of communication is the language
of leadership." - James Humes

Communication is a critical skill for CEOs, as it enables them to convey their vision and strategy to employees, customers, and stakeholders. Effective communication can help build trust, foster collaboration, and drive business success. In this chapter, we will explore the key elements of effective communication for CEOs, and provide practical tips for improving communication skills.

Effective communication begins with listening. CEOs must be willing to actively listen to their employees, customers, and stakeholders in order to understand their perspectives and needs. This involves not only hearing what is being said, but also paying attention to nonverbal cues and asking clarifying questions. By listening attentively, CEOs can build trust, demonstrate empathy, and make informed decisions.

Clarity is essential for effective communication. CEOs must be able to articulate their vision and strategy in a clear and concise manner that is easily understood by all stakeholders. This involves avoiding jargon and technical terms, using simple and direct language, and providing concrete examples to illustrate key points. Clarity also requires tailoring the message to the audience, so that it is relevant and meaningful to each stakeholder group.

Consistency is critical for building trust and credibility. CEOs must ensure that their communication is consistent across all channels and stakeholders, so that everyone receives the same message. This involves aligning communication with the organization's values and vision, and ensuring that all employees are aware of and understand these principles. Consistency also requires following through on commitments and promises, so that stakeholders can rely on the CEO's word.

Transparency is essential for building trust and credibility with employees, customers, and stakeholders. CEOs must be willing to share information and insights openly and honestly, even if it may be uncomfortable or difficult. This involves acknowledging mistakes and shortcomings, providing context for decisions, and being forthcoming about risks and challenges. Transparency also requires being accessible and approachable, so that stakeholders feel comfortable sharing their concerns and feedback.

Effective communication is a two-way process that involves both speaking and listening. CEOs must be willing to engage in dialogue and exchange ideas with employees, customers, and stakeholders in order to build relationships and foster collaboration. This involves encouraging feedback and input, being open to different perspectives and ideas, and responding to questions and concerns in a timely and respectful manner.

Effective communication requires adaptability. CEOs must be able to adjust their communication style and approach to suit the needs of different stakeholders and situations. This involves being aware of cultural and generational differences, understanding the communication preferences of different stakeholder groups, and being flexible in the use of different communication channels. Adaptability also requires being responsive to changing circumstances and adjusting communication accordingly.

Empathy is a critical component of effective communication. CEOs must be able to put themselves in the shoes of their employees, customers, and stakeholders in order to understand their perspectives and needs. This involves actively listening, being open to feedback and input, and demonstrating a willingness to address concerns and issues. Empathy also requires being aware of the emotional impact of communication, and using language and tone that is respectful and supportive.

Effective communication requires ongoing feedback and evaluation. CEOs must be willing to solicit feedback from employees, customers, and stakeholders in order to assess the effectiveness of their communication and make improvements. This involves being open to constructive criticism, actively seeking input, and using feedback to adjust communication and improve relationships.

Effective communication is a critical skill for CEOs, and involves a range of key elements including listening, clarity, consistency, transparency, two-way communication, adaptability, empathy, and feedback. By focusing on these elements and continuously striving to improve communication skills, CEOs can build trust, foster collaboration, and drive business success.

CHAPTER 6: THE IMPORTANCE OF STRATEGIC PLANNING

"Strategy without tactics is the slowest route to victory. Tactics without strategy is the noise before defeat." - Sun Tzu

Strategic planning is the process of defining an organization's direction and making decisions on allocating its resources to pursue this direction. It involves setting goals, developing strategies to achieve those goals, and creating action plans to implement those strategies. Strategic planning is a critical process for any organization, and it is particularly important for CEOs to understand its importance and be involved in the process.

In this chapter, we will explore the importance of strategic planning and its benefits for organizations. We will also discuss the steps involved in the strategic planning process and provide some tips for CEOs to effectively lead their organization through the process.

The Importance of Strategic Planning

Strategic planning is important for several reasons:

Provides a clear direction: Strategic planning provides a clear sense of direction for the organization. By defining the organization's vision, mission, and goals, the organization can focus its resources and efforts towards achieving those goals.

Aligns resources: Strategic planning helps to align the organization's resources, including people, finances, and technology, towards the achievement of the organization's goals. It ensures that resources are used effectively and efficiently to maximize the organization's success.

Anticipates changes: Strategic planning helps the organization anticipate changes in the business environment and adapt to those changes. By regularly reviewing and updating the strategic plan, the organization can respond quickly to changes in the market or industry.

Promotes teamwork and collaboration: Strategic planning involves the participation of multiple stakeholders in the organization, including employees, customers, and partners. This promotes teamwork and collaboration, helping to build a shared sense of purpose and commitment to achieving the organization's goals.

Steps in the Strategic Planning Process

The strategic planning process involves several key steps:

Defining the organization's mission, vision, and values: The first step in the strategic planning process is to define the organization's mission, vision, and values. The mission defines the organization's purpose, while the vision outlines its long-term goals. The values describe the beliefs and principles that guide the organization's actions.

Conducting a SWOT analysis: A SWOT analysis involves analyzing the organization's strengths, weaknesses, opportunities, and threats. This helps the organization to identify its internal strengths and weaknesses, as well as external opportunities and threats.

Setting goals and objectives: Based on the results of the SWOT analysis, the organization can set specific goals and objectives that align with its mission, vision, and values. Goals should be specific, measurable, achievable, relevant, and time-bound (SMART).

Developing strategies: Once goals and objectives have been set, the organization can develop strategies to achieve those goals. This involves identifying the actions and resources required to achieve each goal.

Creating an action plan: An action plan outlines the specific steps required to implement the strategies. It includes timelines, responsible parties, and milestones to track progress towards achieving the goals.

Monitoring and evaluating progress: The final step in the strategic planning process is to monitor and evaluate progress towards achieving the goals. This involves regularly reviewing and updating the strategic plan, and making adjustments as needed to ensure that the organization stays on track.

Tips for CEOs to Effectively Lead the Strategic Planning Process

To effectively lead the strategic planning process, CEOs should:

Involve key stakeholders: The strategic planning process should involve key stakeholders in the organization, including employees, customers, and partners. This helps to build a shared sense of purpose and commitment to achieving the organization's goals.

Set clear expectations: The CEO should set clear expectations for the strategic planning process, including the goals, timelines, and responsibilities for each stage of the process.

Communicate effectively: Effective communication is critical throughout the strategic planning process. The CEO should ensure that all stakeholders are informed of the progress

CHAPTER 7: NAVIGATING CRISIS AND CHANGE AS A CEO

"In the midst of chaos, there is also opportunity." - Sun Tzu

As a CEO, navigating crises and change is an inevitable part of leading an organization. Whether it's a global pandemic, economic downturn, or unexpected industry disruption, CEOs must be prepared to lead their organization through turbulent times. In this chapter, we will explore how CEOs can effectively manage crises and lead their organizations through periods of change.

The best way to manage a crisis is to anticipate it and be prepared for it. While no one can predict the future with complete accuracy, CEOs can take steps to identify potential risks and develop plans to address them. This involves staying informed about industry trends and developments, monitoring external factors that could impact the organization, and conducting scenario planning exercises to identify potential crises and their potential impact.

Once potential crises have been identified, CEOs should develop contingency plans to mitigate their impact. This may involve developing crisis communication plans, establishing protocols for employee safety and security, or identifying alternative suppliers or business partners in case of supply chain disruptions. By taking a proactive approach to crisis management, CEOs can minimize the impact of crises and help their organizations to weather them more effectively.

Effective communication is critical during a crisis. CEOs must be able to communicate quickly and clearly with all stakeholders, including employees, customers, investors, and the media. This involves developing a crisis communication plan that outlines key messages, communication channels, and responsibilities.

During a crisis, it is important for CEOs to be transparent, honest, and empathetic in their communication. They should provide regular updates on the situation and be responsive to questions and concerns. By communicating effectively during a crisis, CEOs can build trust and credibility with stakeholders, and minimize the impact of the crisis on the organization.

Change is inevitable in today's fast-paced business environment. Whether it's a merger, acquisition, restructuring, or new technology adoption, CEOs must be able to lead their organizations through periods of change. This involves being able to communicate a clear vision for the future, inspire and motivate employees, and manage the complexities of change.

To lead through change, CEOs should focus on developing a strong culture of resilience and adaptability within the organization. This may involve providing training and development programs to help employees build new skills, creating a culture of experimentation and innovation, and communicating the benefits of change to all stakeholders.

CEOs must also be able to manage the emotional and psychological aspects of change. Change can be stressful and unsettling for employees, and CEOs must be able to provide support and guidance through the process. This may involve providing regular communication and feedback, creating opportunities for employee input and participation, and recognizing and rewarding employee contributions during the change process.

Resistance to change is a common challenge for CEOs. Employees may resist change due to fear, uncertainty, or a lack of understanding about the benefits of the change. To overcome resistance to change, CEOs must be able to communicate the reasons for the change and address any concerns or objections that employees may have.

One effective approach to overcoming resistance to change is to involve employees in the change process. This may involve creating cross-functional teams to implement the change, providing training and development programs to help employees build new skills, and creating opportunities for employee input and feedback. By involving employees in the change process, CEOs can build buy-in and support for the change, and minimize resistance.

Navigating crisis and change can take a significant emotional toll on CEOs. The stress and pressure of leading an organization through turbulent times can lead to burnout, anxiety, and other mental health challenges. To manage the emotional toll of crisis and change, CEOs must prioritize their own self-care and seek support when needed.

This may involve delegating tasks to other leaders within the organization, practicing stress management techniques like meditation or exercise, and seeking the support of a therapist or coach. It is important for CEOs to recognize the signs of burnout and prioritize their own well-being in order to be effective leaders for their organization.

As a CEO, navigating crises and change is an inevitable part of leading an organization. However, by anticipating and preparing for potential crises, communicating effectively during a crisis, leading through change, overcoming resistance to change, and managing the emotional toll of crisis and change, CEOs can effectively guide their organization through turbulent times. It is important for CEOs to prioritize their own well-being and seek support when needed, in order to be effective leaders for their organization. By successfully navigating crises and change, CEOs can help their organizations to emerge stronger and more resilient than before.

CHAPTER 8: THE IMPORTANCE OF BUILDING A STRONG CORPORATE CULTURE

"The strength of the team is each individual member. The strength of each member is the team." - Phil Jackson

Corporate culture is the set of values, beliefs, and behaviors that shape the way an organization operates. It is an important aspect of any organization, as it influences employee behavior, motivation, and engagement. In this chapter, we will explore the importance of building a strong corporate culture and the strategies that CEOs can use to create a positive and engaging workplace.

Corporate culture is a complex concept that can be difficult to define. At its core, corporate culture is the shared set of values, beliefs, and behaviors that guide how people in an organization think and act. It is the "personality" of an organization and shapes the way employees interact with each other and with external stakeholders.

Corporate culture can be formal or informal. Formal corporate culture is shaped by the organization's leadership and management practices, while informal corporate culture is shaped by the behaviors and attitudes of employees. Both types of corporate culture can have a significant impact on employee engagement, motivation, and productivity.

Corporate culture is important for several reasons. First, it shapes the way employees behave and interact with each other and with external stakeholders. A positive corporate culture can promote collaboration, creativity, and innovation, while a negative corporate culture can lead to conflict, disengagement, and low productivity.

Second, corporate culture is important for attracting and

retaining talent. Employees are more likely to be engaged and motivated when they work in a positive and engaging workplace. A strong corporate culture can help organizations to attract top talent and retain employees over the long term.

Finally, corporate culture is important for achieving strategic goals. A strong corporate culture can help organizations to achieve their strategic objectives by promoting collaboration, innovation, and a sense of shared purpose among employees.

Building a strong corporate culture is a complex process that requires a sustained effort over time. CEOs can use several strategies to create a positive and engaging workplace culture, including:

Defining and communicating core values: Core values are the guiding principles that shape an organization's culture. CEOs should define core values that are aligned with the organization's mission and vision, and communicate them clearly to employees.

Leading by example: CEOs should model the behaviors and attitudes that they want to see in their employees. This involves setting a positive tone at the top and demonstrating a commitment to the organization's core values.

Creating a sense of shared purpose: Employees are more likely to be engaged and motivated when they feel that their work is meaningful and contributes to a larger purpose. CEOs can create a sense of shared purpose by communicating the organization's mission and vision and showing employees how their work contributes to these goals.

Fostering collaboration and teamwork: Collaboration and teamwork are essential for a positive workplace culture. CEOs can promote collaboration by creating cross-functional teams, encouraging communication and feedback, and recognizing and rewarding collaborative behaviors.

Investing in employee development: Employees are more likely to be engaged and motivated when they have opportunities to learn and grow. CEOs can invest in employee development by providing training and development programs, creating opportunities for employees to build new skills, and providing regular feedback and coaching.

Celebrating success: Celebrating success is an important part of building a positive workplace culture. CEOs can recognize and celebrate employee achievements by providing regular feedback and recognition, hosting employee appreciation events, and rewarding employees for their contributions to the organization's success.

Measuring and monitoring corporate culture is essential for building a strong workplace culture. CEOs can use several strategies to measure and monitor corporate culture, including:

Conducting employee surveys: Employee surveys can provide valuable insights into employee attitudes, engagement, and satisfaction. CEOs should use employee surveys to gather feedback on the organization's culture and identify areas for improvement.

Tracking employee turnover: High employee turnover can be a sign of a negative workplace culture. CEOs should track employee turnover rates and use this information to identify potential issues and take steps to address them.

Analyzing performance metrics: Performance metrics, such as productivity, quality, and customer satisfaction, can be a useful indicator of workplace culture. CEOs should analyze these metrics to identify patterns and trends that may indicate issues with workplace culture.

Monitoring social media and online reviews: Social media and online reviews can provide valuable insights into how an organization is perceived by employees and external stakeholders. CEOs should monitor social media and online reviews to identify potential issues and take steps to address them.

Building a strong corporate culture is essential for creating a positive and engaging workplace. CEOs can use several strategies to create a strong workplace culture, including defining core values, leading by example, creating a sense of shared purpose, fostering collaboration and teamwork, investing in employee development, and celebrating success. Measuring and monitoring corporate culture is also important for identifying potential issues and taking steps to address them. By prioritizing corporate culture, CEOs can create a workplace that attracts top talent, promotes innovation, and achieves strategic objectives.

CHAPTER 9: THE POWER OF EFFECTIVE COMMUNICATION IN LEADERSHIP

"Communication is the most important skill any leader can possess." - Richard Branson

Effective communication is a critical skill for leaders in any organization. It enables leaders to articulate their vision and goals, build relationships with stakeholders, and motivate and engage employees. In this chapter, we will explore the power of effective communication in leadership, and the strategies that leaders can use to communicate more effectively.

The Importance of Effective Communication in Leadership

Effective communication is essential for leadership success. It enables leaders to:

Articulate their vision and goals: Effective communication allows leaders to clearly articulate their vision and goals to their stakeholders. By communicating their vision and goals effectively, leaders can inspire their stakeholders and create a sense of purpose and direction for the organization.

Build relationships with stakeholders: Effective communication enables leaders to build strong relationships with their stakeholders, including employees, customers, shareholders, and partners. By communicating openly and honestly, leaders can build trust and credibility with their stakeholders.

Motivate and engage employees: Effective communication is essential for motivating and engaging employees. By communicating effectively, leaders can ensure that employees understand their roles and responsibilities, feel valued and supported, and are aligned with the organization's goals and values.

Navigate change and uncertainty: Effective communication is especially important during times of change and uncertainty. By communicating openly and transparently, leaders can help employees understand why changes are necessary and how they will be affected.

Strategies for Effective Communication in Leadership

Effective communication is a skill that can be learned and developed. Leaders can use several strategies to communicate more effectively, including:

Listen actively: Effective communication starts with active listening. Leaders should listen attentively to their stakeholders, including employees, customers, and partners. Active listening involves paying attention to what the other person is saying, asking clarifying questions, and providing feedback.

Be clear and concise: Effective communication is clear and concise. Leaders should use simple language, avoid jargon and technical terms, and focus on delivering key messages. Clarity is especially important when communicating complex or sensitive information.

Use nonverbal communication: Nonverbal communication, such as facial expressions, gestures, and tone of voice, can convey meaning and emotion. Leaders should pay attention to their nonverbal communication and use it to reinforce their message.

Use multiple channels: Effective communication often involves using multiple channels, such as email, phone, and face-to-face meetings. Leaders should choose the appropriate channel for the message and the audience and use a mix of channels to ensure that the message reaches all stakeholders.

Provide feedback and recognition: Effective communication involves providing feedback and recognition to employees. Leaders should provide regular feedback on performance, recognize and reward good work, and provide opportunities for employees to learn and grow.

Be transparent and honest: Transparency and honesty are essential for effective communication. Leaders should be open and transparent about their vision, goals, and challenges, and be honest about the organization's strengths and weaknesses.

Practice active engagement: Effective communication requires active engagement. Leaders should actively engage with their stakeholders, including employees, customers, and partners, by asking for feedback, listening to concerns, and responding to questions and comments.

The Role of Technology in Effective Communication

Technology can play a powerful role in enabling effective communication in leadership. Leaders can use technology to:

Facilitate remote communication: Technology enables leaders to communicate with stakeholders who are not physically present. Tools such as video conferencing, instant messaging, and collaboration software can facilitate remote communication and collaboration.

Provide real-time feedback: Technology can enable leaders to provide real-time feedback to employees. Tools such as performance management software and instant messaging can facilitate real-time feedback, allowing leaders to provide timely guidance and support.

Enhance communication efficiency: Technology can enhance the efficiency of communication. Tools such as email, messaging apps, and collaboration software can streamline communication processes, allowing leaders to communicate more efficiently with stakeholders.

However, it's important to note that technology should not replace face-to-face communication entirely. While technology can facilitate remote communication and enhance communication efficiency, face-to-face communication remains important for building strong relationships and conveying meaning and emotion.

Challenges to Effective Communication in Leadership

Effective communication is not without its challenges. Leaders may face several barriers to effective communication, including:

Language barriers: In today's globalized business world, language barriers can pose a challenge to effective communication. Leaders should be aware of language barriers and take steps to overcome them, such as providing translations or hiring multilingual employees.

Cultural differences: Cultural differences can also pose a challenge to effective communication. Leaders should be aware of cultural differences and adapt their communication style accordingly.

Perception and bias: Perception and bias can influence how messages are received and interpreted. Leaders should be aware of their own biases and perceptions, as well as those of their stakeholders, and take steps to mitigate them.

Distractions: Distractions, such as noise, interruptions, and technology, can interfere with effective communication. Leaders should minimize distractions during communication and create a distraction-free environment when possible.

Effective communication is a critical skill for leaders in any organization. It enables leaders to articulate their vision and goals, build relationships with stakeholders, and motivate and engage employees. By using strategies such as active listening, clear and concise messaging, nonverbal communication, and transparency, leaders can communicate more effectively. Technology can also play a powerful role in enabling effective communication, but should not replace face-to-face communication entirely.

While challenges to effective communication exist, leaders can overcome them by being aware of language barriers, cultural differences, perception and bias, and distractions. By mastering effective communication, leaders can inspire and motivate their stakeholders, build strong relationships, and drive organizational success.

CHAPTER 10: BUILDING AND LEADING HIGH-PERFORMING TEAMS

"A leader is one who knows the way, goes the way,
and shows the way." - John C. Maxwell

Effective leaders understand that success does not rest on their shoulders alone. Rather, it is a result of the collective efforts of a team. Building and leading high-performing teams is therefore a critical skill for leaders in any organization. In this chapter, we will explore the key elements of building and leading high-performing teams, and the strategies that leaders can use to create and sustain successful teams.

High-performing teams share several key elements that enable them to work together effectively and achieve their goals. These elements include:

Clear goals and expectations: High-performing teams have clear goals and expectations that are aligned with the organization's mission and values. These goals provide a sense of direction and purpose for the team, and enable team members to understand their roles and responsibilities.

Effective communication: Effective communication is essential for high-performing teams. Team members must be able to communicate openly and honestly with one another, share feedback and ideas, and resolve conflicts constructively.

Collaboration and teamwork: High-performing teams collaborate effectively, sharing knowledge and skills to achieve their goals. They work together to solve problems, make decisions, and support one another.

Diversity and inclusion: High-performing teams are diverse and inclusive, valuing the unique perspectives and experiences of all team members. This diversity enables teams to bring a variety of viewpoints and ideas to the table, leading to more innovative solutions.

Continuous learning and development: High-performing teams are committed to continuous learning and development. They seek out opportunities to improve their skills and knowledge, and support one another in their personal and professional growth.

Building high-performing teams requires a deliberate and strategic approach. Leaders can use several strategies to create and sustain successful teams, including:

Clarify goals and expectations: Leaders should ensure that team members understand the team's goals and expectations. This includes setting clear objectives, defining roles and responsibilities, and establishing performance metrics.

Select the right people: Leaders should select team members based on their skills, knowledge, and experience, as well as their fit with the team's culture and values. This includes considering diversity and inclusion in team composition.

Encourage collaboration: Leaders should encourage collaboration and teamwork by providing opportunities for team members to work together, promoting open communication, and fostering a culture of trust and respect.

Provide support and resources: Leaders should provide the necessary support and resources for the team to achieve its goals. This includes providing access to training and development opportunities, as well as the tools and technology needed to do the work.

Celebrate successes: Leaders should celebrate successes and

recognize team members' contributions to the team's achievements. This can include acknowledging milestones, providing incentives and rewards, and publicly recognizing individual and team accomplishments.

Leading high-performing teams requires a unique set of skills and strategies. Leaders can use several approaches to effectively lead their teams, including:

Lead by example: Leaders should model the behaviors they want to see in their team members. This includes demonstrating strong work ethic, effective communication, collaboration, and a commitment to continuous learning and development.

Empower team members: Leaders should empower team members to take ownership of their work and make decisions. This includes delegating responsibilities, providing autonomy, and trusting team members to do their jobs effectively.

Provide feedback and coaching: Leaders should provide regular feedback and coaching to team members. This includes providing constructive feedback on performance, recognizing and celebrating successes, and providing guidance and support as needed.

Encourage innovation and risk-taking: Leaders should encourage team members to take risks and innovate. This includes providing opportunities for experimentation and learning from failures, and creating a culture that values creativity and innovation.

Foster a positive team culture: Leaders should foster a positive team culture that is based on trust, respect, and inclusivity. This includes promoting a sense of belonging and camaraderie among team members, encouraging open communication and collaboration, and actively addressing any conflicts or issues that may arise.

Lead with empathy: Leaders should lead with empathy, taking the time to understand and connect with their team members on a personal level. This includes showing genuine interest in their well-being and supporting them through both professional and personal challenges.

Encourage continuous learning and development: Leaders should encourage continuous learning and development by providing access to training and development opportunities, and promoting a culture of continuous improvement. This includes setting personal and team goals, providing coaching and mentoring, and recognizing and celebrating individual and team growth.

Create a shared vision: Leaders should create a shared vision for the team, aligning it with the organization's mission and values. This includes involving team members in the visioning process, articulating a clear and compelling vision, and ensuring that the team is fully committed to achieving it.

Building and leading high-performing teams is a critical skill for leaders in any organization. High-performing teams share several key elements, including clear goals and expectations, effective communication, collaboration and teamwork, diversity and inclusion, and continuous learning and development. Leaders can use several strategies to build and lead successful teams, including clarifying goals and expectations, selecting the right people, encouraging collaboration, providing support and resources, and celebrating successes.

Effective leadership requires a unique set of skills and strategies, including leading by example, empowering team members, providing feedback and coaching, encouraging innovation and risk-taking, fostering a positive team culture, leading with empathy, encouraging continuous learning and development, and creating a shared vision. By incorporating these strategies and elements into their leadership approach, leaders can create and sustain high-performing teams that achieve their goals and drive organizational success.

CHAPTER 11: EFFECTIVE COMMUNICATION IN THE WORKPLACE

"The single biggest problem in communication is the illusion that it has taken place." - George Bernard Shaw

Effective communication is a critical component of success in any workplace. Whether you are working on a project with colleagues, communicating with clients, or providing feedback to employees, being able to communicate effectively is key to achieving your goals. In this chapter, we will explore the importance of effective communication in the workplace and provide strategies for improving communication skills.

The Importance of Effective Communication

Effective communication is essential in the workplace for a variety of reasons:

Improved productivity: When communication is clear and efficient, employees can work more effectively and efficiently. Misunderstandings and mistakes can be minimized, allowing work to be completed more quickly and accurately.

Better relationships: Effective communication fosters positive relationships among colleagues, managers, and employees. This can lead to increased trust, respect, and collaboration, which can ultimately improve job satisfaction and retention.

Increased innovation: When employees are encouraged to share their ideas and opinions, innovation can thrive. Effective communication allows for the exchange of diverse viewpoints and ideas, leading to more creative solutions and better outcomes.

Better decision-making: When communication is clear and all relevant information is shared, better decisions can be made. Employees can weigh all factors and make informed choices, resulting in better outcomes for the organization.

Strategies for Improving Communication Skills

Improving communication skills requires practice and intentionality. Here are some strategies to help you become a more effective communicator:

Listen actively: Active listening involves paying attention to what the speaker is saying, asking questions, and providing feedback. It shows respect and interest in the speaker and helps ensure that you understand their message.

Use clear and concise language: When communicating, use language that is clear and easy to understand. Avoid using jargon or technical terms that may be unfamiliar to the listener.

Be mindful of body language: Nonverbal communication, such as facial expressions and body language, can convey a lot of information. Be mindful of your own body language and observe others to better understand their messages.

Use appropriate tone and inflection: The tone and inflection of your voice can affect how your message is received. Use a tone and inflection that is appropriate for the message and the audience.

Provide feedback: Provide feedback to others in a constructive and supportive manner. Use specific examples and provide suggestions for improvement.

Practice empathy: Empathy involves understanding and sharing the feelings of others. Practice empathy by putting yourself in the other person's shoes and considering their perspective.

Use technology wisely: Technology can be a valuable tool for communication, but it can also be a hindrance. Use technology wisely by choosing the most appropriate medium for the message and being mindful of tone and context.

Follow up: Following up on communication is important to ensure that messages are understood and goals are achieved. Follow up with colleagues, clients, or employees to ensure that all parties are on the same page.

Tips for Communicating with Different Audiences

Effective communication requires tailoring your message to your audience. Here are some tips for communicating with different audiences:

Colleagues: When communicating with colleagues, use professional language and be mindful of tone and body language. Focus on the task at hand and be respectful of their time and responsibilities.

Clients: When communicating with clients, focus on building relationships and providing excellent customer service. Use language that is clear and concise, and be responsive to their needs and concerns.

Managers: When communicating with managers, focus on providing information that is relevant to their role and responsibilities. Use data and examples to support your message, and be prepared to provide solutions to any problems or challenges.

Employees: When communicating with employees, be transparent and honest. Provide clear expectations and feedback, and be available to answer questions and provide support. Be approachable and foster an environment where employees feel comfortable sharing their ideas and concerns.

Barriers to Effective Communication

Despite our best efforts, communication can sometimes break down or be hindered by various barriers. Here are some common barriers to effective communication in the workplace:

Language barriers: Language differences can make it difficult to communicate effectively with coworkers or clients who speak a different language. This can result in misunderstandings or misinterpretations of information.

Cultural differences: Cultural differences can also lead to misunderstandings or miscommunications. Different cultures may have different communication styles, which can lead to confusion or offense if not understood.

Emotional barriers: Emotions can also act as a barrier to effective communication. If an individual is upset or emotional, it can be difficult to communicate effectively, as emotions may cloud judgment and affect the delivery or interpretation of messages.

Technological barriers: Overreliance on technology can also be a barrier to effective communication. If individuals are not familiar with certain technology or if the technology malfunctions, communication may be hindered.

Overcoming Communication Barriers

To overcome communication barriers, it is important to identify and address them as soon as possible. Here are some strategies for overcoming communication barriers in the workplace:

Language barriers: If language barriers are present, consider using translation tools or hiring an interpreter. Additionally, simplifying language and avoiding technical jargon can also help improve understanding.

Cultural differences: To overcome cultural differences, it is important to learn about different communication styles and practices. This can include researching different cultures or asking for feedback and input from colleagues or clients from different cultural backgrounds.

Emotional barriers: When emotions are high, it may be necessary to take a break and revisit the conversation at a later time. Practicing active listening and empathy can also help defuse emotional situations.

Technological barriers: To overcome technological barriers, it may be necessary to provide training or resources to help individuals become more comfortable with technology. Additionally, having a backup plan in case of technology malfunctions can help ensure that communication can continue.

Effective communication is crucial for success in any workplace. By actively listening, using clear language, being mindful of body language and tone, practicing empathy, and using technology wisely, individuals can improve their communication skills. Additionally, tailoring communication to different audiences and addressing barriers to effective communication can help foster positive relationships, increase productivity, and drive innovation. By prioritizing effective communication, individuals can contribute to a more successful and productive workplace.

CHAPTER 12: CONFLICT RESOLUTION IN THE WORKPLACE

"In the middle of every difficulty lies opportunity." - Albert Einstein

Conflict is a natural part of any workplace, but it can also be a source of stress and tension. When conflict is not resolved, it can lead to decreased productivity, low morale, and high turnover rates. In this chapter, we will explore the importance of conflict resolution in the workplace and provide strategies for effectively managing conflict.

Conflict resolution is essential in the workplace for several reasons:

Improved productivity: Conflict can be a major distraction in the workplace. When conflicts are resolved, employees can focus on their work and be more productive.

Better relationships: Resolving conflicts in a respectful and productive manner can improve relationships among colleagues, managers, and employees. This can lead to increased trust, respect, and collaboration, which can ultimately improve job satisfaction and retention.

Increased innovation: When conflicts are resolved, employees can focus on creative problem-solving and innovative solutions. This can lead to better outcomes and improved performance.

Reduced stress: Unresolved conflict can be a significant source of stress in the workplace. When conflicts are resolved, employees can feel a greater sense of peace and comfort in their work environment.

Strategies for Managing Conflict

Managing conflict effectively requires skill and practice. Here are some strategies for effectively managing conflict in the workplace:

Identify the Source of the Conflict: To resolve a conflict, it is important to identify the source of the conflict. This can involve identifying the underlying issues, emotions, and goals of each party involved in the conflict.

Listen Carefully: Listening is a critical part of conflict resolution. Active listening involves paying attention to what the other person is saying, asking questions, and summarizing what you have heard. This shows respect and interest in the other person's perspective.

Communicate Clearly: Clear communication is essential in conflict resolution. Use clear and concise language, avoid blaming or accusing language, and be mindful of your tone and body language.

Focus on Solutions: When resolving a conflict, it is important to focus on solutions rather than the problem itself. This involves brainstorming potential solutions and working collaboratively to find a resolution that meets the needs of all parties involved.

Be Flexible: Flexibility is an important part of conflict resolution. Be open to different perspectives and solutions, and be willing to make concessions in order to reach a resolution.

Maintain Professionalism: Maintaining professionalism is critical in conflict resolution. Avoid personal attacks or insults, stay focused on the issue at hand, and avoid getting emotional or defensive.

Seek Mediation: In some cases, seeking mediation may be

necessary to resolve a conflict. A mediator can help to facilitate communication, identify underlying issues, and guide parties toward a resolution.

Effective conflict management requires adapting your approach to different settings. Here are some tips for managing conflict in different settings:

Colleagues: When conflicts arise among colleagues, it is important to remain professional and respectful. Focus on the issue at hand and avoid personal attacks or insults.

Clients: Conflict with clients can be particularly challenging. It is important to remain calm, listen carefully, and focus on finding a solution that meets the needs of both parties.

Managers: When conflicts arise with managers, it is important to remain respectful and professional. Focus on finding a solution that meets the needs of both parties, and be willing to compromise when necessary.

Employees: When conflicts arise with employees, it is important to remain transparent and honest. Be clear about your expectations, provide constructive feedback, and work collaboratively to find a solution.

Strategies for Preventing Conflict

While conflict is a natural part of any workplace, there are strategies that can be used to prevent conflicts from occurring. Here are some strategies for preventing conflict in the workplace:

Establish Clear Expectations: Setting clear expectations and guidelines for behavior and performance can help prevent misunderstandings and conflicts in the workplace. Make sure all employees understand their roles and responsibilities, as well as the expectations for communication and collaboration.

Encourage Open Communication: Encouraging open communication can help prevent conflicts from escalating. Make sure employees feel comfortable sharing their concerns and feedback with each other and with management. Consider holding regular team meetings to facilitate open communication and collaboration.

Promote Team Building: Team building activities can help foster positive relationships and trust among employees. Consider organizing team-building exercises, social events, or other activities that allow employees to get to know each other outside of work.

Provide Training and Development: Providing training and development opportunities can help employees develop the skills they need to effectively manage conflicts. Consider offering training on effective communication, problem-solving, and conflict resolution.

Address Issues Early: Addressing issues early can help prevent conflicts from escalating. When a potential conflict arises, take the time to address it promptly and respectfully. This can help prevent the conflict from becoming more serious or damaging relationships.

Conflict is a natural part of any workplace, but it is essential to manage it effectively. Resolving conflicts can lead to improved productivity, better relationships, increased innovation, and reduced stress. Effective conflict resolution requires identifying the source of the conflict, listening carefully, communicating clearly, focusing on solutions, being flexible, maintaining professionalism, and seeking mediation when necessary. Preventing conflicts from occurring requires establishing clear expectations, encouraging open communication, promoting team building, providing training and development, and addressing issues early. By implementing these strategies, organizations can create a more positive and productive work environment for all employees.

CHAPTER 13: EFFECTIVE TIME MANAGEMENT IN THE WORKPLACE

: "Time is what we want most, but what we
use worst." - William Penn

Time management is an essential skill for success in the workplace. Effective time management allows employees to prioritize tasks, meet deadlines, and achieve goals efficiently. In this chapter, we will explore the importance of time management in the workplace and provide strategies for effective time management.

Effective time management is crucial in the workplace for several reasons:

- Increased productivity: Good time management skills can help employees be more productive, allowing them to accomplish more tasks in less time.

- Better work-life balance: Effective time management can help employees balance their work responsibilities with their personal life, reducing stress and improving overall well-being.

- Reduced stress: Poor time management can lead to missed deadlines and unfinished tasks, causing stress and anxiety. Effective time management can reduce these negative emotions and improve mental health.

- Improved job satisfaction: When employees are able to manage their time effectively, they are more likely to feel a sense of accomplishment and job satisfaction.

Strategies for Effective Time Management

Effective time management requires planning and prioritization.

Here are some strategies for effective time management:

Set Priorities: Setting priorities is an essential part of effective time management. Determine which tasks are most important and focus on those first.

Make a Schedule: Create a schedule that outlines your tasks and when they need to be completed. This can help you stay on track and ensure that you meet deadlines.

Avoid Procrastination: Procrastination can be a major barrier to effective time management. Identify tasks that you tend to procrastinate on and develop strategies for addressing these tendencies.

Eliminate Distractions: Distractions can be a significant obstacle to effective time management. Identify potential distractions and develop strategies for minimizing them.

Delegate Tasks: Delegating tasks to others can help you manage your time more effectively. Determine which tasks can be delegated and identify colleagues who can assist.

Take Breaks: Taking regular breaks can help you stay focused and productive. Take short breaks throughout the day to recharge and refocus.

Use Technology: Technology can be a useful tool for effective time management. Use digital calendars, reminder apps, and other tools to stay organized and on schedule.

Effective time management requires adapting your approach to different settings. Here are some tips for effective time management in different settings:

Office: In an office setting, it is important to create a schedule and prioritize tasks. Eliminate distractions by closing your office door, turning off notifications, and avoiding unnecessary meetings.

Remote Work: When working remotely, it is important to set clear boundaries between work and personal life. Create a schedule that allows time for breaks and personal activities.

Meetings: Meetings can be a major drain on time and productivity. Set an agenda, keep meetings focused, and avoid unnecessary meetings.

Travel: When traveling for work, it is important to plan ahead and make the most of your time. Use travel time to catch up on work tasks, listen to podcasts or audiobooks, or prepare for meetings.

Strategies for Preventing Time Management Issues

Effective time management requires proactive measures to prevent potential issues. Here are some strategies for preventing time management issues in the workplace:

Set Realistic Goals: Setting unrealistic goals can lead to feelings of failure and stress. Set achievable goals that align with your schedule and resources.

Communicate with Others: Communicating with colleagues and managers can help prevent time management issues. Discuss priorities, deadlines, and schedules to ensure that everyone is on the same page.

Manage Expectations: Managing expectations is an important part of effective time management. Be clear about what you can realistically accomplish within a given timeframe.

Track Your Time: Tracking your time can help you identify patterns and areas where you can improve your time management skills.

Take Care of Yourself: Taking care of your physical and mental health is an important aspect of effective time management. Eat well, exercise regularly, and get enough sleep to ensure that you have the energy and focus you need to be productive.

Learn to Say No: Saying yes to every request or task can quickly lead to a feeling of overwhelm and poor time management. Learn to say no when necessary and prioritize tasks that are most important.

Review and Reflect: Regularly reviewing and reflecting on your time management strategies can help you identify areas for improvement and make necessary changes.

Effective time management is essential for success in the workplace. By prioritizing tasks, making a schedule, avoiding procrastination, eliminating distractions, delegating tasks, taking breaks, and using technology, employees can manage their time more efficiently and reduce stress.

Adapting time management strategies to different settings, preventing potential issues, and taking care of oneself are also important aspects of effective time management. By implementing these strategies and making time management a priority, employees can achieve their goals and enjoy a more balanced work-life.

CHAPTER 14: DECISION MAKING

"Decisions made at the right time are the most
effective decisions." - John C. Maxwell

One of the most critical skills that a CEO must possess is the ability to make effective decisions. Decision making is a complex process that involves weighing options, assessing risks, and evaluating potential outcomes. The decisions made by a CEO can have a significant impact on the success or failure of a company, making it imperative for them to have a thorough understanding of the decision-making process.

The ability to make sound decisions is a crucial factor in the success of any CEO. It is the CEO's responsibility to make strategic decisions that will determine the direction of the company. CEOs must be able to analyze data, anticipate market trends, and evaluate risks in order to make informed decisions that will benefit the organization. Effective decision making also helps a CEO to build a positive reputation and maintain the trust of stakeholders, such as shareholders and employees.

There are several factors that can influence a CEO's decision-making process. Some of these factors include:

Emotional Bias: Emotions can impact a CEO's ability to make rational decisions. Fear, anxiety, and stress can cloud judgment and lead to poor decision making.

Cognitive Biases: Cognitive biases can also impact decision making. Confirmation bias, where a CEO only considers information that confirms their pre-existing beliefs, can lead to poor decisions.

Time Constraints: CEOs are often under pressure to make quick decisions. This can lead to hasty decisions that are not well thought out.

Company Culture: The culture of a company can impact decision making. In some organizations, there may be pressure to conform to a certain way of thinking or decision making style.

There are many examples of successful and unsuccessful decisions made by CEOs. One example of a successful decision is when Steve Jobs, the former CEO of Apple, decided to launch the iPod. At the time, there were already many MP3 players on the market. However, Jobs saw an opportunity to create a superior product that would revolutionize the industry. The iPod became a massive success and helped to solidify Apple's position as a leader in the technology industry.

On the other hand, one example of an unsuccessful decision is when John Sculley, the former CEO of Apple, decided to fire Steve Jobs in 1985. Sculley believed that Jobs was too focused on product development and not enough on profitability. However, Jobs' vision and leadership had been instrumental in the success of the company up to that point. Jobs went on to start his own company, NeXT, and eventually returned to Apple and helped to turn the company around.

Strategies for Effective Decision Making

There are several strategies that a CEO can use to improve their decision-making skills. Some of these strategies include:

Analyze Data: Analyzing data can provide valuable insights that can help a CEO make informed decisions. CEOs should gather as much data as possible and analyze it carefully before making a decision.

Consider Different Perspectives: It is important to consider different perspectives when making decisions. This can help a CEO to see the bigger picture and avoid cognitive biases.

Seek Input from Others: Seeking input from other team members can help a CEO to make more informed decisions. It can also help to build trust and foster collaboration within the organization.

Anticipate Risks: It is important to anticipate potential risks when making decisions. CEOs should consider all possible outcomes and evaluate the potential risks and rewards of each option.

Evaluate the Decision: After making a decision, it is important to evaluate its effectiveness. This can help a CEO to learn from their mistakes and improve their decision-making skills in the future.

Effective decision making is a crucial skill that every CEO must possess . The ability to make informed decisions can determine the success or failure of a company. CEOs must understand the factors that influence their decision making, such as emotional and cognitive biases, time constraints, and company culture. By analyzing data, considering different perspectives, seeking input from others, anticipating risks, and evaluating decisions, CEOs can improve their decision-making skills and make sound choices for their organizations.

It is important for CEOs to learn from both successful and unsuccessful decisions. Steve Jobs' decision to launch the iPod is an excellent example of a successful decision that helped Apple become a leader in the technology industry. However, John Sculley's decision to fire Steve Jobs is an example of an unsuccessful decision that had long-lasting negative consequences for Apple. CEOs must carefully consider the potential outcomes of their decisions and be willing to take calculated risks to achieve their goals.

Effective decision making is an ongoing process that requires continuous learning and improvement. CEOs must be open to feedback and willing to evaluate the effectiveness of their decisions. By developing strong decision-making skills, CEOs can build a positive reputation, maintain the trust of stakeholders, and guide their organizations to success.

CHAPTER 15: WORK-LIFE BALANCE

"Happiness is not a matter of intensity but of balance, order, rhythm and harmony." - Thomas Merton

CEOs are known for their busy schedules and demanding work hours, which can make it difficult to maintain a healthy work-life balance. However, striking a balance between work and personal life is crucial for the well-being of a CEO, both professionally and personally. In this chapter, we will explore the challenges faced by CEOs in achieving work-life balance and strategies for maintaining it.

CEOs are expected to be constantly available and responsive, which can create a blur between work and personal life. It is essential for CEOs to set boundaries and allocate time for personal life activities like hobbies, exercise, and family. Personal time can help a CEO recharge and maintain mental and emotional well-being, which can ultimately enhance work productivity.

The biggest challenge faced by CEOs in achieving work-life balance is time management. CEOs are expected to prioritize business demands over personal time, which can lead to burnout, stress, and decreased job satisfaction. The pressure to meet business objectives can also lead to neglecting personal relationships and health, which can have a negative impact on personal well-being.

To achieve a healthy work-life balance, CEOs can adopt strategies such as delegation, time management, and setting priorities. Delegation can help distribute responsibilities and allow CEOs to focus on higher priority tasks, while time management can help optimize daily schedules and reduce time spent on unproductive activities. Setting clear priorities can help CEOs allocate time and resources effectively and prevent unnecessary stress.

In addition, CEOs can also adopt practices such as mindfulness, regular exercise, and adequate sleep to enhance personal well-being and reduce stress. Seeking support from family, friends, and colleagues can also help create a support system and promote a healthy work-life balance.

Achieving a healthy work-life balance is essential for CEOs to maintain personal well-being, job satisfaction, and productivity. By adopting effective time management strategies and prioritizing personal time, CEOs can achieve a balance between work and personal life, ultimately leading to better overall performance.

CHAPTER 16: LEADERSHIP STYLE OF A CEO

"Great leaders are willing to sacrifice their own personal interests for the good of the team." - John Wooden

A CEO's leadership style can greatly impact the success of a company. There are several different leadership styles that a CEO can adopt, including autocratic, democratic, transformational, and servant leadership.

An autocratic leadership style involves a CEO who makes decisions without input from their team. This can be effective in situations where quick decision-making is necessary, but it can also lead to low morale and resentment from team members.

A democratic leadership style involves a CEO who involves their team in decision-making processes. This can lead to increased motivation and job satisfaction for team members, but can also be time-consuming and slow down decision-making processes.

Transformational leadership involves a CEO who inspires their team and leads by example. This style can be effective in motivating teams to achieve a common goal, but can also lead to burnout if the CEO is unable to balance their own workload while leading by example.

A servant leadership style involves a CEO who prioritizes the needs of their team and works to serve them. This can lead to increased trust and loyalty from team members, but can also be challenging if the CEO is unable to balance the needs of their team with the needs of the company.

It is important for a CEO to understand their own leadership style and how it affects their team. A CEO who is able to adapt their leadership style to fit the situation at hand is more likely to be successful in leading their team to success.

There are several examples of successful CEOs with different leadership styles. Steve Jobs, the co-founder of Apple, was known for his autocratic leadership style, while John Mackey, the co-founder of Whole Foods, is known for his servant leadership style. Jeff Bezos, the founder of Amazon, has been known to adopt a transformational leadership style, while Tim Cook, the CEO of Apple, is known for his democratic leadership style.

Ultimately, a CEO's leadership style should be chosen based on the needs of the company and the team. By understanding the strengths and weaknesses of different leadership styles, a CEO can make informed decisions about how to lead their team to success.

CHAPTER 17: MANAGING A TEAM

"To handle yourself, use your head; to handle others, use your heart." - Eleanor Roosevelt

A CEO's leadership style is closely linked to how they manage their team. In this chapter, we'll explore the key aspects of managing a team, including building a strong team, the challenges faced in managing a team, and strategies for effective team management.

A CEO's success is largely dependent on the strength and cohesion of their team. To build a strong team, a CEO must first establish clear goals and expectations. This involves setting the tone for the company's culture and values, which should be reflected in the team's behavior and decision-making.

Next, a CEO must hire the right people for the job. This involves identifying the skills, experience, and personality traits required for each role, and selecting candidates who meet these criteria. It's important to consider not only a candidate's qualifications, but also their fit within the team and their potential for growth and development.

Once a team is in place, a CEO must focus on building relationships with their team members. This involves open communication, regular feedback and recognition, and creating opportunities for team members to collaborate and learn from one another.

Managing a team is not without its challenges. Some of the most common issues CEOs face include managing conflict, dealing with underperforming team members, and keeping team morale high during difficult times.

Conflict can arise when team members have different priorities, opinions, or approaches to work. A CEO must be able to mediate conflicts and find solutions that are satisfactory for all parties involved.

Underperforming team members can be a drain on the team's productivity and morale. A CEO must be able to identify the root cause of underperformance and work with the team member to address it. This may involve providing additional training or resources, setting clearer expectations, or redefining the team member's role.

Finally, team morale can suffer during periods of change or uncertainty, such as a merger or acquisition, a change in leadership, or a downturn in the market. A CEO must be able to maintain team morale by communicating openly and honestly, providing support and resources, and leading by example.

To effectively manage a team, a CEO must focus on building trust, fostering collaboration, and providing direction and support. Here are some key strategies for effective team management:

- Communicate regularly and transparently with your team
- Provide regular feedback and recognition
- Encourage collaboration and open communication
- Set clear expectations and hold team members accountable
- Provide opportunities for learning and development
- Lead by example and model the behavior you expect from your team

Managing a team is a crucial aspect of a CEO's job. Building a strong, cohesive team, managing conflicts, and maintaining team morale are essential for achieving success. Effective team management requires a combination of leadership skills, communication, and a focus on building relationships with team members.

CHAPTER 18: CORPORATE SOCIAL RESPONSIBILITY

"Corporate social responsibility is not a cost,
it's a strategy." - Simon Mainwaring

Corporate social responsibility (CSR) refers to the initiatives taken by a company to ensure its operations have a positive impact on society and the environment. As a CEO, implementing CSR initiatives is not only the right thing to do but also has several benefits for the company. In this chapter, we will explore the definition and importance of CSR, as well as examples of successful initiatives taken by CEOs.

Definition of corporate social responsibility

CSR involves taking responsibility for the impact a company's operations have on society and the environment. It includes efforts to minimize negative impacts, such as pollution and waste, as well as initiatives to create positive social and environmental outcomes, such as supporting local communities and promoting sustainable practices.

Importance of corporate social responsibility for a CEO

Implementing CSR initiatives can have several benefits for a company, including enhancing the company's reputation, increasing employee satisfaction and retention, attracting socially conscious customers, and improving relationships with stakeholders such as regulators, suppliers, and investors.

As a CEO, being seen as a responsible corporate citizen can enhance the company's brand, which can lead to increased sales and customer loyalty. It can also help to attract and retain employees who are passionate about making a positive impact on society and the environment.

Examples of successful corporate social responsibility initiatives by CEOs

There are many examples of successful CSR initiatives implemented by CEOs. For example, Patagonia CEO Yvon Chouinard has been a vocal advocate for sustainable business practices and environmental conservation. The company has implemented several initiatives, including using organic cotton in its clothing, donating 1% of its sales to environmental causes, and launching a campaign to encourage customers to repair and reuse their clothing.

Another example is Starbucks CEO Howard Schultz, who has implemented several CSR initiatives, including sourcing coffee beans from sustainable sources, providing education and training to coffee farmers, and launching a program to hire refugees.

As a CEO, implementing CSR initiatives can have several benefits for the company, including enhancing the company's reputation and attracting socially conscious customers and employees. By taking responsibility for the impact the company's operations have on society and the environment, CEOs can demonstrate their commitment to being a responsible corporate citizen.

CHAPTER 19: NETWORKING

"Your network is your net worth." - Porter Gale

Networking is an essential skill for any CEO. A CEO's network can help them gain new business, access funding, find new talent, and learn about new opportunities. In this chapter, we will explore the importance of networking for a CEO and provide strategies for building a strong network.

Importance of networking for a CEO

Networking is critical for a CEO because it allows them to make connections with other professionals, potential clients, and stakeholders. A strong network can help a CEO build credibility, access new business opportunities, and gain insights into industry trends. Networking can also provide a CEO with a support system and a sounding board for new ideas and challenges.

Building a strong network

Building a strong network takes time and effort. A CEO should be intentional about attending networking events, conferences, and industry meetings. They should also leverage social media platforms, such as LinkedIn, to connect with other professionals in their field. A CEO should also focus on building authentic relationships and adding value to their network by sharing knowledge and resources.

Examples of successful networking by CEOs

Many successful CEOs are known for their strong networking skills. For example, Richard Branson, the founder of Virgin Group, is known for his ability to connect with people from all walks of life. Branson attends numerous industry events and makes it a priority to build relationships with other entrepreneurs and business leaders. Similarly, Oprah Winfrey, the founder of OWN, is known for her ability to build a strong personal brand and leverage her network to gain new business opportunities.

An example of a CEO with exceptional networking skills is Jack Ma, the founder of Alibaba. Ma is known for his ability to navigate complex relationships and build connections with important business leaders and government officials in China. He is also known for his charismatic personality and willingness to take risks, which has helped him to build a strong network of supporters and collaborators.

Another successful CEO who is known for his networking skills is Bill Gates, the founder of Microsoft. Gates has an extensive network of contacts in the technology industry and is often sought after for his expertise and insights. Gates is also known for his philanthropic efforts, which have helped him to build relationships with other leaders in the non-profit sector.

In addition to these examples, successful CEOs across various industries understand the importance of networking and building relationships with others. They attend industry events, participate in conferences and seminars, and leverage social media platforms to connect with other professionals. By building a strong network, CEOs can gain valuable insights, identify new business opportunities, and establish themselves as leaders in their respective industries.

Networking is a critical skill for any CEO. Building a strong network takes time and effort, but the benefits of having a strong network can be invaluable. CEOs should focus on building authentic relationships and adding value to their network by sharing knowledge and resources. By doing so, they can gain insights into industry trends, access new business opportunities, and build a support system to help them navigate the challenges of being a CEO.

CHAPTER 20: MAINTAINING A POSITIVE REPUTATION

"It takes 20 years to build a reputation and five minutes to ruin it. If you think about that, you'll do things differently." - Warren Buffett

In today's business world, a positive reputation is critical for a CEO's success. A positive reputation can help a CEO attract top talent, secure new business opportunities, and maintain the trust of stakeholders. On the other hand, a negative reputation can quickly erode a CEO's credibility and damage their company's brand.

Importance of a Positive Reputation for a CEO

A positive reputation is important for a CEO because it helps build trust with stakeholders. Customers, investors, employees, and the general public are more likely to support a CEO and their company if they have a positive reputation. In addition, a positive reputation can help a CEO attract top talent, as potential employees are more likely to want to work for a company with a good reputation.

Another benefit of a positive reputation is that it can help a CEO secure new business opportunities. Partnerships and collaborations with other companies are more likely to occur if a CEO has a good reputation. Additionally, a positive reputation can make it easier for a CEO to secure funding for their company's growth and expansion.

Strategies for Maintaining a Positive Reputation

Maintaining a positive reputation is not an easy task, but there are strategies that CEOs can implement to help ensure they are seen in a positive light by stakeholders.

Firstly, transparency is key. Being transparent with stakeholders helps build trust and credibility. CEOs should communicate openly and honestly with stakeholders, particularly during times of crisis. A CEO who is transparent about their company's challenges and how they are addressing them is more likely to be seen in a positive light.

Secondly, a CEO should be mindful of their public image. This means being aware of their actions both in and outside of the workplace. A CEO's behavior can have a significant impact on their reputation. For example, if a CEO is known for making controversial statements or engaging in unethical behavior, it can quickly damage their reputation.

Thirdly, a CEO should focus on providing value to stakeholders. This means prioritizing the needs of customers, employees, and investors above their own personal interests. A CEO who is seen as putting the needs of stakeholders first is more likely to be respected and trusted.

Examples of Successful Reputation Management by CEOs

There are many examples of CEOs who have successfully managed their reputation. For example, Tim Cook, the CEO of Apple, has been praised for his efforts to improve the company's social and environmental impact. Cook has implemented a number of initiatives to reduce Apple's carbon footprint and improve working conditions for employees.

Another example is Mary Barra, the CEO of General Motors. Barra was faced with a crisis when it was discovered that faulty ignition switches in GM vehicles had caused multiple deaths. Barra responded to the crisis by being transparent and taking responsibility for the company's mistakes. She also implemented changes to improve the company's safety procedures.

On the other hand, there are also examples of CEOs who have struggled with reputation management. For example, Travis Kalanick, the former CEO of Uber, was criticized for his behavior towards employees and customers. His aggressive leadership style and lack of transparency led to a negative perception of the company and ultimately his resignation.

Maintaining a positive reputation is critical for a CEO's success. CEOs should focus on being transparent, mindful of their public image, and providing value to stakeholders. By doing so, they can build trust with stakeholders and maintain a positive reputation that will benefit their company in the long run.

CHAPTER 21: CONCLUSION

"The greatest leaders are not necessarily the ones who do the greatest things. They are the ones who inspire others to do great things." - Ronald Reagan

As we come to the end of "The Secret Life of a CEO," it's important to reflect on the key points and takeaways from this book. Throughout the book, we have explored various aspects of a CEO's life, from their early life and development of leadership skills to effective communication, strategic planning, crisis management, and work-life balance.

One of the most important themes that emerged throughout the book was the importance of effective communication in all aspects of a CEO's life. Communication skills are essential for building and maintaining a strong company culture, leading high-performing teams, resolving conflicts, and making sound decisions.

Another key theme was the importance of a CEO's leadership style. The book highlighted the different types of leadership styles that CEOs can adopt, and emphasized the importance of choosing a style that suits their personality, strengths, and goals.

We also explored the importance of work-life balance, which can be a significant challenge for CEOs who have demanding jobs that require them to work long hours and manage a wide range of responsibilities. However, we also discussed various strategies that CEOs can use to achieve a balance between work and personal life, such as prioritizing self-care and delegating tasks to others.

Corporate social responsibility emerged as another important theme in the book. We explored the concept of corporate social responsibility and the ways in which CEOs can use their companies to make a positive impact on the world. We also looked at several examples of successful CSR initiatives by CEOs, including efforts to reduce carbon emissions, support social justice causes, and promote diversity and inclusion in the workplace.

Finally, we discussed the importance of maintaining a positive reputation as a CEO. A CEO's reputation can have a significant impact on their company's success, and it's essential for CEOs to develop strategies for managing their reputation effectively. We looked at examples of successful and unsuccessful reputation management by CEOs, and discussed various strategies for building and maintaining a positive reputation.

"The Secret Life of a CEO" offers a comprehensive guide to the challenges and opportunities faced by CEOs. By exploring the key themes of effective communication, leadership style, work-life balance, corporate social responsibility, and reputation management, this book provides aspiring CEOs with the tools and strategies they need to succeed in their roles. We hope that this book has been a valuable resource for anyone interested in the world of CEOs, and we wish all aspiring CEOs the best of luck in their careers.